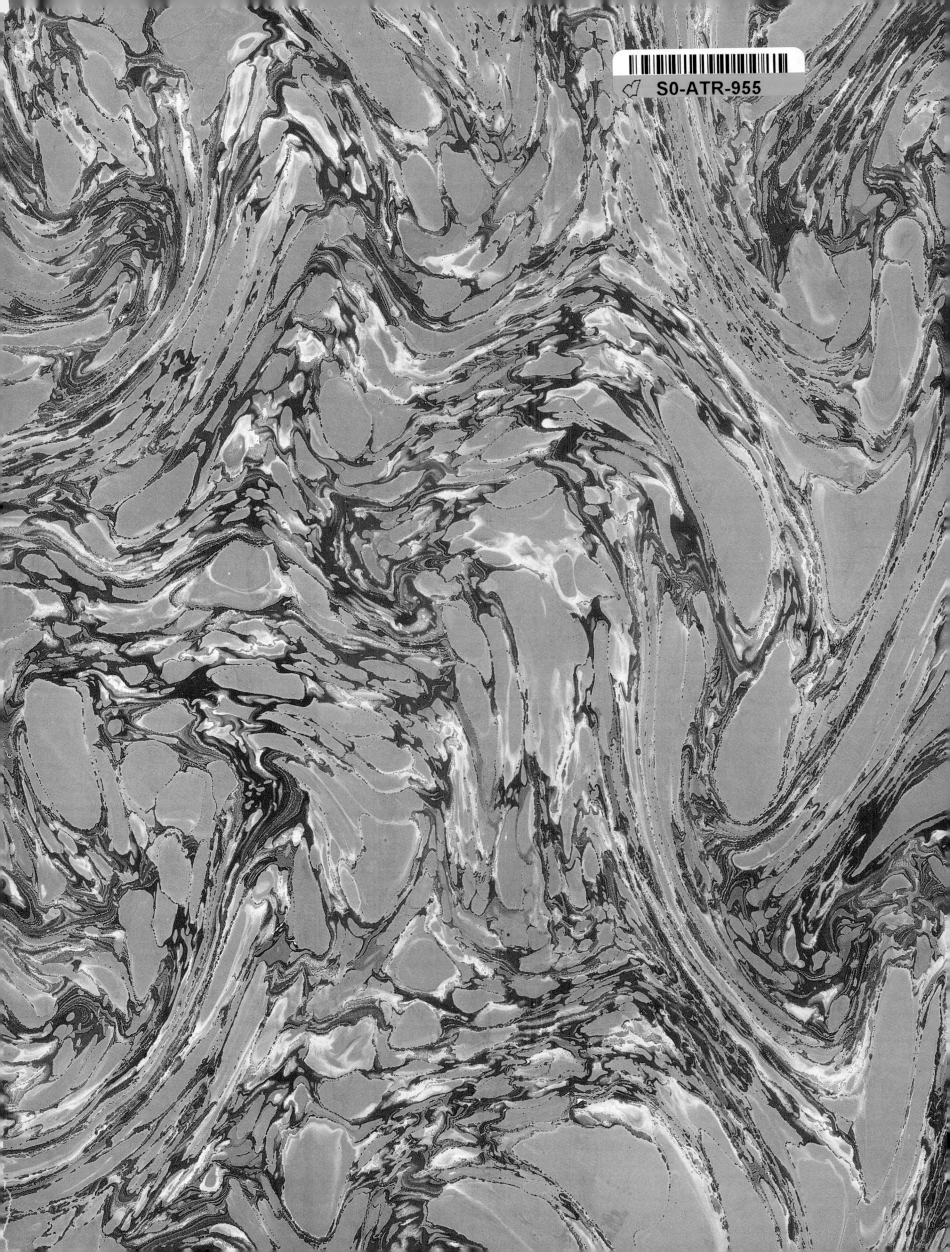

YOSEMITE ILLUSTRATED IN COLORS

YOSEMITE

ILLUSTRATED IN COLORS

1890

WINDGATE PRESS : SAUSALITO, CALIFORNIA

Published by Windgate Press
P.O. Box 1715, Sausalito, CA 94966

Printed in Korea by Sung In America.
FIRST EDITION

ISBN 0-915269-23-6

Foreword:

ON REPRINTING THE 1890 EDITION OF
YOSEMITE, ILLUSTRATED IN COLORS

THE ORIGINAL 1890 edition of *Yosemite, Illustrated in Colors* was part of a successful effort by prominent Californians to promote creation of a national park encompassing Yosemite Valley. This handsome work, published in San Francisco by H.S. Crocker Company, California's preeminent printer, was the earliest "coffee table" book illustrating the wonders of Yosemite. Printed in color, it achieved a remarkable level of quality for its time. Today, original copies are scarce, sought after by antiquarian book collectors.

The book was a product of its era, when the Yosemite Valley had been accessible via coach roads for less than twenty years. Only thirty-five years had passed since the first lithographs of Yosemite had been published. Most Americans had not visited the new national park, and only a small percentage had seen paintings or any visual representation of it in color. *Yosemite, Illustrated in Colors* served for several years after 1890, in various editions, to promote and popularize Yosemite. Not only did it represent the transformation of Yosemite from a wilderness to a recreational park, it helped set the public perception of Yosemite that exists today.

Until 1890, most published graphic depictions of Yosemite were black and white lithographs and wood engravings that emphasized the valley's dramatic, wild character. Yosemite was shown as spectacular but forbidding and dangerous, with precipitous rocky crags, gorgeous primeval cataracts, a place of grizzly bears. Even the early photographs by Carleton E. Watkins, Eadweard Muybridge, and others reveal a magnificent but somewhat less than inviting Yosemite. In *Yosemite, Illustrated in Colors*, the famous waterfalls and rock formations are bucolic and non-threatening, the valley floor is hospitable and harmonious, a place of recreation, camping, hunting and fishing.

Yosemite, Illustrated in Colors deserves to be seen again. Its vivid chromolithographs retain the power to charm and captivate as they did over a century ago. This new edition of *Yosemite, Illustrated in Colors* faithfully reproduces the twelve plates of Yosemite landmarks. Included also is the original descriptive text by Warren Cheney, augmented by the late-Victorian romantic poems composed by Harry Dix for the original edition.

L. Witwer
Windgate Press

CONTENTS

Sentinel Rock, Bridal Veil,
El Capitan, The Cascades, The Three Brothers,
Vernal Fall, Cathedral Spires, Nevada Fall,
Cathedral Rock, Yosemite Falls,
The Half Dome, General View

Original Water Color Sketches	by H.W. Hansen.
Original Oil Sketches	by Carll Dahlgren.
Pen and Ink Sketches	by H.W. Hansen.
Text	by Warren Cheney.
Poems	by Harry Dix.
Originally Lithographed	by H.S. Crocker & Co., San Francisco.

ILLUSTRATIONS

Preface
to the 1890 Edition

THE YOSEMITE VALLEY is at once a satisfaction and an inspiration. It is the one place which entirely fulfills the expectation of the observer. No one has ever seen it without receiving from it the lasting impression of moral elevation which comes from the near association with the sublimer manifestations of nature. It is the greatest of the natural wonders of California; but it is unique only in the point of size. There are in the State a half-dozen other valleys exactly similar in formation and structure, which present, in a smaller way, like wonders of cataract and cliff; but nowhere else in the whole world is there such a marvelous aggregation of stupendous crags and dizzy waterfalls as is gathered together in this strange Sierran gorge. The valley has been known to white men for almost forty years; but, long before that time, its existence was no secret to the Indians of the section, who occupied it as a dwelling-place and a fortress, and appreciatively designated, by legend and appropriate name, every point of interest that attracts the tourist of today. The romantic story of its discovery, the mysterious and boastful statements of the Indians concerning its supernatural quality and infinite inaccessibility, the massacre at Savage's store, the hurried pursuit, the treaty with Ten-ie-ya, the broken promise, and the final descent into the valley, these are matters of history, and do not call for more than mention here. But although four decades have passed since that little body of soldiers first looked down into the Yosemite, the valley has been really known and visited for much less than half that time. It was five years after the discovery before the first real effort at exploration was made. The character of the times was such, the nature of the population so nomadic and practical, that for a long time its beauties and its marvels were far better known in other lands than on the Pacific Coast. The first tourists, therefore, were largely foreigners; but, as the local population grew, there came to be an ever-increasing number of those who were willing to brave the hardships of the long, dusty ride over the sun-parched plains, the weary travel through the inaccessible mountains in which it lay, and the risk to life and limb that came with the breathless climb over the primitive valley trails. Today the Yosemite is as easy to reach as the smoky cone of Vesuvius or the Rigi-Kulm. All the year round there is a stream of curious sightseers entering or passing out through its gates. There is no class of people that is not reached by its fascination and interested by its charms. A thousand new species of strange plants and shrubs attract the interested eyes of the botanist; and the scientist has found infinite food for suggestion in its geologic forms, and has quarreled to his heart's content over the manner of its formation. At first it was supposed to be an instance of what is technically called a "slip;" that during some mighty convulsion of nature the bottom suddenly dropped out at the point where the valley now is, and the whole mass of rock detritus went down a dizzy mile to the level of the present valley floor. A careful examination, however, of the formation of the vertical sides, the long parallel scratches that show the handwriting of the moving ice, the smoother surfaces turned to the lower valley, the splitting of the cañon at its head, and the rounded moulding of the overhanging domes, all proclaim the fact that the Yosemite was in reality hollowed out by the irresistible, grinding force of some vast prehistoric glacier.

Since we commenced this work the Fifty-first Congress has passed two laws of vast importance to lovers of natural beauty. It has withdrawn the Big Tree Grove of Tulare county from settlement and has passed the Yosemite National Park Bill, immensely extending the boundaries of the Yosemite Grant.

The new National Park takes in the entire drainage area of the Yosemite, and much more. It embraces the whole of the upper Tuolumne river, with the Hetch Hetchy valley and the greater part of the Tuolumne water shed. It includes Mount Lyell and its glaciers, Lake Eleanor, and the Mariposa, Merced and Tuolumne groves of Big Trees. It stretches from Lake Eleanor to Wawona and beyond, and from Hazel Green below Crane Flat to the highest ridge of the Sierra. It is about fifty miles in length by thirty-five in width, and considerably exceeds the State of Rhode Island in area.

This magnificent reservation will be by far the most beautiful park in the world. It will lack the weird marvels of the Yellowstone — the geysers, the painted rocks and stalagmitic formation — but in the magnificence and charm of forest, cliff and waterfall, it will be beyond comparison. It will give a new impetus to the tide of Yosemite travel.

SENTINEL ROCK.

SOMEWHAT beyond Cathedral Rock, and on the same side of the valley, rises the majestic needle of stone which is known as Sentinel Rock, or the Sentinel. It is an imposing obelisk towering a sheer thousand feet above the rock wall on which it stands, and lifting its head a full three thousand feet above the valley. It is the great central landmark of the place. From its top not only is every nook and cranny of the valley in full view, but the range of vision takes in all the county bordering on its walls for many miles around. The Indians were throughly familiar with this fact; and, long before white men had ever set foot in the valley, they named it *Loya*, the sentinel, and established a lookout station for military purposes on its crest. Now it is seldom climbed, as the ascent is very difficult, and no better view of the valley can be had from it than is obtained from other points more easily reached. But it will always remain one of the notable objects of interest in the place; for, whether seen direct or in the beautiful river reflection, its clear-cut lines and majestic height make it more than usually prominent in the landscape.

The Sentinel.

Oh, Loya, thou who proudly stands

    Deserted in the might,

Once watchful eyes of savage bands

    Kept guard upon thy height.

Not always have thy walls of stone

Such peacefulness and silence known.

Few, few there are who reach thy crest,

    For long and steep the climb;

But he who scales thy rugged breast

    Is well repaid the time.

The valley wide beneath his gaze

Its every storied charm displays.

BRIDAL VEIL.

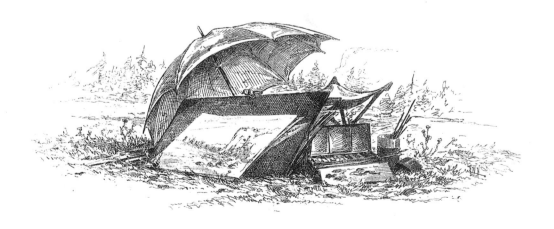

BEFORE the threshold of the valley is passed, falling from the top of the great cliff that forms one lintel of the doorway is Bridal Veil Fall, the first cataract to arrest the attention of the observer going in. For a time it is hard to believe that it is a waterfall at all, so unlike is it to anything one is accustomed to associate with that name. From its plunge over the face of the cliff to its disappearance in the tumbled rocks below it is simply a filmy, shifting web of vapor, tinted by the sunlight with all the colors of the rainbow, and changing momentarily with the fancy of the wind. At times it swings back and forward across the face of the cliff with the sweep and motion of a majestic pendulum. Then the current produced by its own rushing passes behind and under it, pushing it up till it lies like a crumpled veil against the summit of the rock. Often it floats out entirely free of the base, like an enormous pennant; and its spray settles down in soft gray clouds, which roll like mist along the levels. So fine is this subdivision of the spray, that the sheer drop of a thousand feet is made by the water in comparative silence. It is this silence, coupled with the fleecy quality of the foam, which has won for it the name of the Bridal Veil; and truly no web more delicate or more richly colored ever came from the famed looms of the East.

The Bridal Veil.

A veil of spray, a rush, a tide

Of water down the mountain side,

A torrent ever flashing bright,

And sparkling in the sunbeams' light.

A moving river fed with snow

To fall a thousand feet below.

A foaming mass the traveler sees,

The sport of every passing breeze.

With clouds of mist that fall and rise

Like vapor from the burdened skies,

Or pennant floating on the gale,

Such is the fall of "Bridal Veil."

El Capitan.

L CAPITAN (the captain), is the name given to the stupendous square-cut, granite mass which forms the left-hand portal to the valley. Clean-cut and treeless it rises abruptly from the base, its imposing head being a sheer three thousand feet above the river. It is the overshadowing genius of the place. It is visible from the San Joaquin Valley a hundred miles away. It fronts you as you catch the first glimpse of the Yosemite from Inspiration Point. It leans its projecting head above you as you pass the gateway in entering below. It grows continually larger and more majestic as you move away from it beyond. Its presence cannot be escaped. No matter where the view be taken, its dignified vastness is always in the landscape. In the sun it is creamy white, shading away in long shadows through browns to the deepest black. It is the sun dial of the valley. Long before it is sunrise on the river levels, the light begins to whiten on its crest. And as the hour advances the shore line of shadow on its face—the surface edge of the flood of dusk which still pervades the valley—slips slowly and regularly downward toward its base, till the gorge is drained of the darkness and the sunlight touches the meadows at its foot.

El Capitan.

A treeless cliff that from its base

    Does upward rise three thousand feet,

    As though it would the heavens meet.

And stands the Genius of the place;

A rock upon whose rugged face

    The first faint arrows of the sun

    Tell of another day begun,

And mark the records of its race.

    A weird, majestic mass of gray

    That fronts you, gaze where'er you may.

THE CASCADES.

CONSPICUOUS and all-absorbing as are the great falls and precipices of the Yosemite, there is also within its precincts a multitude of minor heights and cataracts which would not fail to attract attention were it not for the proximity of their grander neighbors. One of these lesser attractions is the stream which pours its flood over the cliff between El Capitan and the narrow mouth of the cañon to the west, and which, from the succession of plunges made in the descent to the valley, has received the name of The Cascades. It is an ever-changing succession of broken falls, which flash in and among the huge blocks of granite, making now a quiet eddying pool, and now a stretch of foam of dazzling whiteness. Two streams on the upper level flowing in from diametrically opposite directions join just before reaching the brink and lend their combined volumes to form the torrent. In the descent of seven hundred feet there is an infinite variety of bounding waters which surge and swirl and dash and leap, til with a final plunge the stream lands in a beautiful green meadow, across which it flows to the Merced in a bright and sparkling flood. The beauty of the spot is greatly enhanced by the thick growth of nutmeg, live-oak and pine which covers the face of the cliff.

The Cascades.

Softly, the cataract, sparkling, transparent,

      Darts like a falling star over the cliff;

Swiftly it plunges, then dashes adown the glen

      Over the mighty crags, fallen and rift.

Oh, for its energy, wild and untiring,

      Never it wearies or changes its song.

Loudly the echoes roll back from the granite wall

      Where the swift crystal flood hurries along.

Over the jagged rocks, white from a hundred shocks,

      Down til the field it meets, rushes the tide;

Down for five hundred feet, down til the meadows sweet

      With their rank grasses deep spread on each side.

THE THREE BROTHERS.

LMOST all of the Indian names for points of interest in the Yosemite are more appropriate and interesting than their later Christian christenings. Especially good was the cognomen given by these "first inhabitants" to the tri-cleft rock now known as the Three Brothers. *Pom-pom-pa-sa* they called it, "the mountains playing leap-frog;" and it does not require a vivid imagination to understand their reason for giving it this name. There is a curious and easily discernible resemblance between the rocks and a series of frogs sitting close behind each another; and the uplifted, pointed heads, together with the angle at which they rise, gives them the appearance of being about to leap. The modern name was given in commemoration of the capture of the three sons of the old Indian Chief Ten-ie-ya, which occurred at this point during the campaign of 1851. The rock is interesting in its variety, being so entirely different in structure and appearance from any other formation in the valley. Its highest peak rises three thousand eight hundred and eighteen feet above the roadway. A beautiful view on the road near Rocky Point is obtained of the entire eastern end of the valley.

The Three Brothers.

Three monuments recall the name

    Of those who held Yosemite

Long years before the white men came

    And led them to captivity.

The one above the other stands,

    A stony ladder upward driven,

As if to reach those hunting lands

    That are the Indian warrior's heaven.

Within the shadows at the base

    Ten-ie-ya saw his sons enchained,

And with the remnant of his race

    The mountain's secret fastness gained.

VERNAL FALL.

VARIOUS effects in color have combined to exemplify in the Vernal Fall the significance of its name. The water itself is a peculiar transparent shade of green; the ferns and lichens that cover the rocks along its sides are wet continually with the rising spray, and sparkle with a spring-like freshness of color; and the base of the fall is hidden by a growth of fir and spruce, through the deeper green of whose leaves the cataract is seen from below framed as in a picture. It is the quietest and most beautiful fall in the valley, and brings no sense of awe in its companionship. It is so perfectly accessible and takes its four hundred feet of plunge with such calmness and lack of flurry that one feels perfectly sure it will do its work properly without his cooperation, and can give his whole attention to consideration of its beauty. Above the fall there is a long stretch of quiet water; and it begins its leap over the edge of a square table of rock so flat that one can lie at length and drink of the water after it has left the brink. Ladder-like steps lead down by the right-hand side, by which descent may be made into the mist-swept slippery cañon below. From this point the view of the fall is especially fine, as the sunlight builds bow upon bow of colors over the water from base to the very summit of the rock.

Vernal Fall.

Over the mountain wall so steep

Down to the rocks the waters leap,

Cover with foam the mosses deep

    And sparkle in the sun.

Splashing the bending forms with spray,

Washing over the lichens gray,

Ever the waters take their way—

    Ever and ever run.

Holding the rainbow's dazzling light,

Spinning along in restless flight,

Through the noontide into the night,

    Yet never, oh never, done.

CATHEDRAL SPIRES.

OUT of the extreme right hand corner of the great Cathedral Rock—so far, indeed, that they cannot be seen till after the gateway of the valley is passed—rise the two needle-like columns of rock which serve as spires to that fictitious church. In reality, they are quite widely separated ; but so small is the distance between them, as compared with the great height at which one views them from below, that they seem to stand close together and rise from a common pediment of rock. There is a difference of about a hundred feet in their height—the northern peak being the smaller. The southern measures seven hundred feet from base to apex. The beauty of both lies in their slender, tapering, needle-like shape. Seen from a distance, their naked faces seem perfectly smooth and rounded. A close inspection, however, shows that the wind and weather have worn them to an uneven granular structure. Myriads of little points stand out in low relief, and their facets have a wonderful power of absorbing and reflecting the sunlight, which gives—in the early morning especially—an almost luminous quality to the rock.

The Spires.

The evening sun is sinking fast

    Behind the mount and hill,

But oh, upon Cathedral Spires

    Her glory lingers still;

A thousand shining points retain

    The splendor of her ray,

And flash and signal back again

    The parting smile of day.

Like arrows shot into the sky

    From some almighty bow,

So rise these stony shafts on high

    And shade the vale below.

NEVADA FALL.

NATURE has arranged the surroundings of the Nevada Fall with a special eye to its appreciation. Not only is the scenery about it particularly picturesque, but, being in the upper cañon, it is out of sight of the other wonders of the valley, and holds the full attention of the observer. It is sufficiently remarkable in itself, however, to dispense with these accessories. It is the one fall that divides one's allegiance with the Yosemite. The great volume of water, the long drop of over seven hundred feet, the marvelous and ever-shifting play of colors over its surface, and the deafening tumult of sound that comes up incessantly from its basin, all combine in suggesting the same sensations of sublimity and beauty that are afforded by a consideration of its greater rival. It has, too, the same peculiar manner of fall. The water seems to separate into a thousand jets or streams, like a great flight of downward shooting rockets, which mingle and remingle in endless variety and plan, until at the base they are swallowed up in the solid stream of the river. The cliff over which the fall takes its leap is not quite perpendicular; and the inequities on its face so turn the current that it comes down with a peculiar sidewise, shifting motion. In recognition of this fact, the Indians appropriately called this fall *Yo-wi-ye*, or the Great Twisted Water.

Nevada Fall.

Dashing, splashing, moving ever,

    Shifting, shooting rocket-like,

Down they pour to join the river,

With a rushing and a quiver,

    As the bursting of a dike.

Now they part and now uniting,

Now a thousand streams are fighting

    In the changing of the light,

And the hissing water columns

Fling away the foam in volumes—

    Onward to eternity

Leap the rapid twisted waters,

    Drop the falls of "Yo-wi-ye."

CATHEDRAL ROCK.

THERE is a marked difference between the cliffs that form the portals to the valley. El Capitan is so rugged and imposing, so clear-cut and distinctive in color, that is somewhat overshadows its neighbor across the threshold. But the rock mass on the right has also its notable characteristics. It is more graceful and more shapely, more spiritual and more suggestive of things connected with human life. So close does it compare, both in proportion and design, with some great gothic building, that it has received the name of the Cathedral Rock. It has the same air lightness in its vertical lines, and is braced here and there, along its base, with high - reaching gothic buttresses of stone. The resemblance to a church is still further carried out by two graceful pinnacles of rock which crown its summit, and serve in place of spires. It is a cathedral for the gods, however, for its roof is twenty-seven hundred feet above its base. The space immediately around it is thickly wooded, and, here and there, on a ledge or in a crevice, a tree or bush has taken root, and hangs against the face like a sailor clinging to the shrouds. But, practically, the purity of surface is not interfered with, and these spots of color serve to relieve the dullness of the rock and gather delightful contrasts of light and shade.

Cathedral Rock.

With stately air and graceful mien,

    With columns high and Gothic frame,

    There rises from the valley, plain

Above the landscape broad and green,

    A rock-hewn fane of sculptured stone

    That ne'er an altar priest hath known.

A temple with a hidden shrine

    Where nature, in her majesty,

    Is the all-ruling deity;

Where water-falls and storms combine

To sing an anthem most divine.

YOSEMITE FALL.

OSEMITE FALL is the largest and most impressive cataract in the valley. All waterfalls have their distinctive characteristics; and this one might well be taken as the synonym of sublimity and force. There is about it none of the delicacy and softening that idealizes the vision of the Bridal Veil; nor the quietness and wealth of color that makes of the Vernal a living type of beauty. It is a half mile of boisterous, whirling, falling water rushing headlong down the cliff with such a mad hurry of incessant motion that, looking at it, everything is forgotten but the irresistible sensation of its dynamic power. It is twenty-seven hundred feet high, and from below appears a single unbroken fall. But looked at from the side it is seen to be divided into a succession of cascades. Its first dizzy leap is over sixteen hundred feet; but between this and the next direct descent there is a quarter mile of tumbling rapids. Then comes a plunge of six hundred feet checked by the rocky oval of a basin its own fury has hollowed in the granite, and after that the final leap of five hundred to the valley floor. Its sound is like the varying reverberations of continued thunder. So great is the volume of descending water, and so intense the impetus of it s fall, that a steady draught of air is lifted like a mighty wind from the cauldron of black rocks at its base, which beats upon the observer with a force that almost sweeps him from his feet.

Yosemite Falls.

Vast protégé of nature, thou who pours

        Thy silken waves like waters from the sky,

Thou snow-fed champion,– thou who roars

        And lives while centuries pass and die.

Thy waters are the high Sierra's veins,

        Thy falls their offering, and thy noise their song.

The thunder of thy columns shakes the plains

        And roll their echoes through the hills along.

Thy breath is as the ice-king's withering blast,

        Thy strength is as the current of the sea.

Men seem as pygmies in thy presence vast,

        And time takes nought from thy sublimity.

THE HALF DOME.

IN ALL the world there is nothing similar to the Half Dome of the Yosemite. Whole domes are not an uncommon feature of mountain scenery. But this great peak is like some well-rounded mosque roof cleft cleanly in twain, as if by a sword or some sharp instrument. From behind, except by height, it could not be distinguished from its neighbor on the north. All that is visible is its steep curve growing more abrupt as it descends, and the creamy glint of its overlapping granite scales. From the valley side, however, there is nothing to hide the wonderful height of its vertical face. Almost a mile it rises sheer above the river. The upper two thousand feet is absolutely perpendicular and the remainder slopes but slightly out into the valley. The whole front is of smooth and weather-polished stone; and no *débris* lies at the bottom to suggest that its precipitousness resulted from a falling of the rock. On its top is a comparatively level place of some seven acres in extent where a few stunted trees are found. Otherwise, aside from occasional lichen streaks, it is absolutely bare, and over and around, from top to bottom, of one even tint of yellow gray.

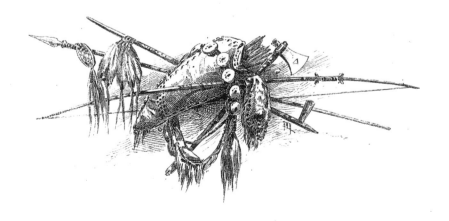

The Half Dome.

I climbed the mountain with its summit tall,

    O'er rugged rocks that lead up to the dome,

Just as the sun's bright fiery ball

    Had sunk beneath the circle of my zone;

And from the surface of its barren crown

    I gazed in wonder at the landscape wide,

Where torrents rose and fell and rivers wound

    In tortuous windings by the mountain side.

An awe, a feeling of the power that made

    And formed and blended all the great in one,

Passed through me, and I stood, like one afraid,

    On heights which catch the full force of the sun.

The lapping rock, the granite's mosque-like dome,

    With all around, is Nature's, Nature's own.

General View.

GRAND as is the view of the Yosemite Valley from Artist's Point, the immensity of the distances traversed by the eye relieves the sense of awful height and depth, and gives the impression of beauty equally with sublimity. Tremendous is the only adjective that entirely expresses this wonderful gorge. But from this point its spaces are so filled with softening haze, that the impression is as if one saw the scene mirrored in a Lorraine glass and not as an actual reality in nature. It is a view of peak and precipice rather than of cataract; for, with the exception of the Bridal Veil, which flutters like a snowy pennant from the right-hand gateway of the valley, none of the larger falls are distinctly visible. Four thousand feet below is the green floor of the valley, with the Merced winding through it like a silver thread. Directly opposite, looking through two miles of air, one sees the farther granite wall, clean cut and bare, and marked with a winding scroll-like line that is the other road leading down into the valley. Beyond El Capitan the cañon widens into the valley proper, affording the vista of one great peak after another in endless variety of form and characteristic. At the narrowing head the view is closed by the sharp-cut oval of the great South Dome, and beyond this the white-mitered crest of Clouds Rest with its everlasting snows, the advance picket of the perpetual ice fields which lie just beyond it to the East.

General View.

Look from this point, and lo your sight

    Will fall on heights and dizzy peaks

Where heaven burns her signals bright

    And Nature her communion seeks.

        If you would view God's works, go see

        The Valley of Yosemite.

And high, how high and grand they rise,

    their summits as you near them seem

To pierce the dome of arching skies

    And vanish in the clouds between.

        For grandeur, grace and beauty see

        The Valley of Yosemite.

Look further, range on range appears

    Divided now by chasms wide,

With forests ancient as the years

    And streams that cut the mountain side.

        Oh wondrous, dread immensity.

        Oh Valley of Yosemite.

HUTCHINGS HOTEL — SENTINEL ROCK IN THE DISTANCE. — John S. Davis.

CREATION OF A PARK

The wood engraving opposite, "Hutchings' Hotel" by John S. Davis, illustrates the gradual transformation of Yosemite from a pristine wilderness to a popular recreation area. The struggle to preserve the valley and protect it from destructive exploitation began soon after its discovery by non-Indian explorers in the 1830s and 1840s. When the Indians were driven out of the valley, conservation-minded Californians feared an influx of prospectors and settlers into the valley would destroy its fragile nature. After California gained statehood in 1850, it wasn't long before influential Californians urged the federal government to preserve Yosemite Valley's natural wonders. Congress in 1864 set aside Yosemite Valley and the Mariposa Grove of Big Trees, granting the lands to the state of California in perpetuity.

The act of 1864, however, permitted commercial leases of property within the valley to promote "public use, resort, and recreation." By 1878, when the wood engraving opposite was made, five hotels operated in Yosemite, with more on the way. The valley saw its first saloon and billiard hall open for business. Permanent residents of Yosemite were numerous enough to create a school district by 1876. Hundreds of square miles of wilderness surrounding Yosemite Valley had no protection from exploitation. Ranchers grazed sheep and cattle in the valley and the upper meadows, a practice that threatened the natural flora and fauna. Conservationists feared that Yosemite, as it attracted more people, was in danger and needed broader protection.

Over the next two decades, the tireless efforts of many, including conservationist John Muir, resulted in Congressional action. Yosemite National Park was created in 1890, encompassing over 1,500 square miles surrounding Yosemite Valley. The 1890 act also set aside the lands that became General Grant National Park and Sequoia National Park. In 1906, after more pressure and lobbying, the original 1864 grant of the valley to California was rescinded, and Yosemite Valley was merged into the surrounding lands of the national park.

Following are the texts of the congressional acts that laid the foundation for today's national park, along with an 1872 map showing the relative location of Yosemite Valley's best known features.

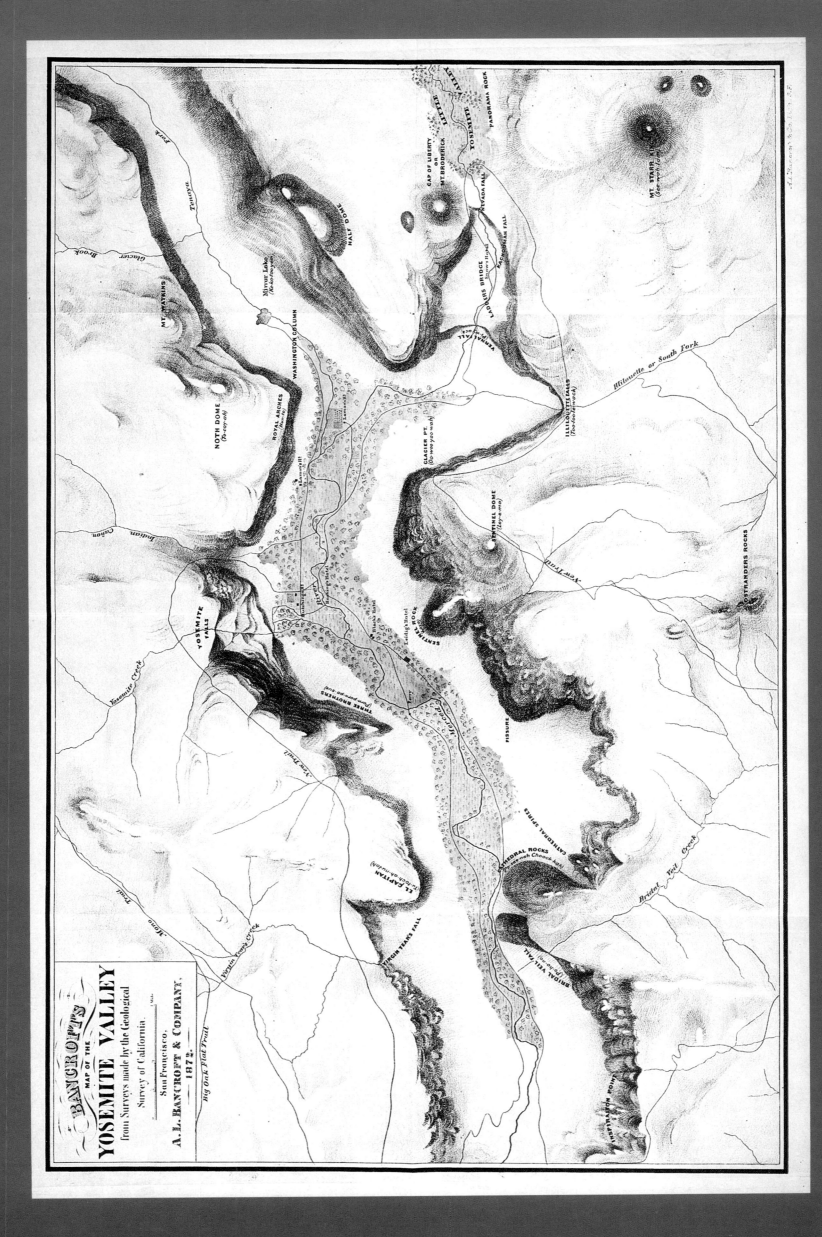

BANCROFT'S
MAP OF THE
YOSEMITE VALLEY
from Surveys made by the Geological
Survey of California.
San Francisco,
A. L. BANCROFT & COMPANY,
1872.

AN ACT

AUTHORIZING A GRANT TO THE STATE OF CALIFORNIA OF THE "YO-SEMITE VALLEY," AND OF THE LAND EMBRACING THE "MARIPOSA BIG TREE GROVE."

SEC.I. *Be it enacted by the Senate and House of Representatives of the United States of America in Congress assembled,* That there shall be, and is hereby, granted to the State of California the "Cleft" or "Gorge" in the granite peak of the Sierra Nevada mountains, situated in the county of Mariposa, in the State aforesaid, and the headwaters of the Merced River, and known as the Yo-Semite valley, with its branches or spurs, in estimated length fifteen miles, and in average width one mile back from the main edge of the precipice, on each side of the valley, with the stipulation, nevertheless, that the said State shall accept this grant upon the express conditions that the premises shall be held for public use, resort and recreation; shall be inalienable for all time; but leases not exceeding ten years may be granted for portions of said premises. All incomes derived from leases of privileges to be expended in the preservation and improvement of the property, or the roads leading thereto; the boundaries to be established at the cost of said State by the United States surveyor-general of California, whose official plat, when affirmed by the commissioner of the general land-office, shall constitute the evidence of the locus, extent, and limits of the said Cleft or Gorge; the premises to be managed by the governor of the State with eight other commissioners, to be appointed by the executive of California, and who shall receive no compensation for their services.

SEC.2. *And be it further enacted,* That there shall likewise be, and there is hereby, granted to the said State of California the tracts embracing what is known as the "Mariposa Big Tree Grove," not to exceed the area of four sections, and to be taken in legal sub-divisions of one quarter section each, with the like stipulation as expressed in the first section of this act as to the State's acceptance, with like conditions as in the first section of this act as to inalienability, yet with the same lease privilege; the income to be expended in preservation, improvement, and protection of the property; the premises to be managed by commissioners as stipulated in the first section of this act, and to be taken in legal sub-divisions as aforesaid; and the official plat of the United States surveyor-general, when affirmed by the commissioner of the general land-office, to be the evidence of the locus of the said Mariposa Big Tree Grove.

Approved by Congress, June 30, 1864

Abraham Lincoln
President of the United States

An Act

TO SET APART CERTAIN TRACTS OF LAND IN THE STATE OF CALIFORNIA AS FOREST RESERVATIONS.

SEC. I. *Be it enacted by the Senate and House of Representatives of the United States of America in Congress assembled,* That the tracts of land in the State of California known as described as follows:

> Commencing at the northwest corner of township two north, range nineteen east Mount Diablo meridian, thence eastwardly on the line between townships two and three north, ranges twenty-four and twenty-five east; thence southwardly on the line between ranges twenty-four and twenty-five east to the Mount Diablo base line; thence eastwardly on said base line to the corner to township one south, ranges twenty-five and twenty-six east; thence southwardly on the line between ranges twenty-five and twenty-six east to the southeast corner of the township two south, range twenty five east; thence eastwardly on the line between townships two and three south, range twenty-six east to the corner to townships two and three south, ranges twenty-six and twenty-seven east; thence southwardly on the line between ranges twenty-six and twenty-seven east to the first standard parallel south; thence westwardly on the first standard parallel south to the southwest corner of township four south, range nineteen east; thence northwardly on the line between ranges eighteen and nineteen east to the northwest corner of township two south, range nineteen east; thence westwardly on the line between townships one and two south to the southwest corner of township one south, range nineteen east; thence northwardly on the line between ranges eighteen and nineteen east to the northwest corner of township two north, range nineteen east, the place of beginning,

Are hereby reserved and withdrawn from settlement, occupancy, or sale under the laws of the United States, and set apart as reserved forest lands; and all persons who shall locate or settle upon, or occupy the same or any part thereof, except as hereinafter provided, shall be considered trespassers and removed therefrom: *Provided, however,* That nothing in this act shall be construed as in anywise affecting the grant of lands made to the State of California by virtue of the act entitled "An act authorizing a grant to the State of California of the Yosemite Valley, and of the land embracing the Mariposa Big -Tree Grove, approved June thirtieth, eighteen hundred and sixty-four; or as affecting any bona-fide entry of land made within the limits above described under any law of the United States prior to the approval of this act

SEC. 2. That said reservation shall be under the exclusive control of the Secretary of the Interior, whose duty it shall be, as soon as practicable, to make and publish such rules and regulations as he may deem necessary or proper for the care and management of the same. Such regulations shall provide for the preservation from injury of all timber, mineral deposits, natural curiosities, or wonders within said reservation, and their retention in their natural condition. The Secretary may, in his discretion, grant leases for building purposes for terms not exceeding ten years of small parcels of ground not exceeding five acres; at such places in said reservation as shall require the erection of buildings for the accommodation of visitors; all of the proceeds of said leases and other revenues that may be derived from any source connected with said reservation to be expended under his direction in the management of the same and the construction of roads and paths therein. He shall provide against the wanton destruction of the fish, and game found within said reservation, and against their capture or destruction, for the purposes of merchandise or profit. He shall cause all persons trespassing upon the same after the passage of this act to be removed therefrom, and, generally, shall be authorized to take all such measures as shall be necessary or proper to fully carry out the objects and purposes of this act.

SEC. 3. There shall also be and is hereby reserved and withdrawn from settlement, occupancy or sale under the laws of the United States, and shall be set apart as reserved forest lands, as herein before provided, and subject to all the limitations ands provisions herein contained, the following additional lands, to wit;

Township seventeen, south, range thirty east of the Mount Diablo meridian, excepting sections thirty-one, thirty-two, thirty-three, and thirty-four of said township, included in a previous bill. And there is also reserved and withdrawn from settlement, occupancy or sale under the laws of the United States, and set apart as forest lands, subject to like limitations, conditions and provisions, all of townships fifteen and sixteen, south, of ranges twenty-nine and thirty east of the Mount Diablo meridian. And there is also hereby reserved and withdrawn from settlement, occupancy or sale under the laws of the United States, and set apart as reserved forest lands under like limitations, restrictions and provisions, Sections five and six in township fourteen, south, range twenty-eight, east of Mount Diablo meridian, and also Sections thirty-one and thirty-two of township thirteen, south, range twenty-eight east of the same meridian.

Nothing in this act shall authorize rules or contracts touching the protection and improvement of said reservations, beyond the sums that may be received by the Secretary of the Interior under the forgoing provisions, or authorize any charge against the Treasury of the United States.

Approved by Congress, October 1, 1890

Benjamin Harrison
President of the United States

As Yosemite became more widely known and attracted more visitors, guide books and descriptions for the tourist appeared. This 1881 booklet poses the question, "which is the best route?" By then, at least three stage roads led into the valley. The map inserted in the booklet illustrates the advantages of the Big Oak Flat Road that offers side trips to the Calaveras big trees. By 1907, railroad service from San Francisco and other points to El Portal, at the entrance to Yosemite Valley, offered even greater convenience. And, by 1915, visitors could drive their automobiles right into the valley. In the 1860s visitors to Yosemite numbered about seven hundred annually. By 1907, the number had risen to around two thousand per year. Today, over 4,000,000 people a year visit Yosemite National Park.

Opposite: The Nelson Pictorial Guide Book from 1881, shown actual size, was illustrated with color lithographs and distributed nationwide as well as in Europe. Between 1864 and 1890, "Yo-Semite" evolved into the modern spelling, "Yosemite." Other place names in the valley have undergone slight transformations as well. "Bridal Veil Fall," for example, has become "Bridalveil Fall."

THE YO-SEMITE VALLEY.
(From the Mariposa Trail.)

NELSONS PICTORIAL GUIDE BOOKS

SCENERY OF CALIFORNIA

THE BIG TREES AND THE YOSEMITE VALLEY

T. NELSON & SONS   NEW YORK

SOUVENIR BOOKLET AND PLATES, 1881.

THE NORTH & SOUTH DOMES.
(Yo-semite Valley.)

Sentinel Rock and Fall.

Perhaps the most widely distributed early images of Yosemite Valley were those contained in *Picturesque America*, first published in 1874. The seven-hundred-page, heavily illustrated volume was immensely popular and remained in circulation for almost thirty years. It became a visual frame of reference for many Americans who otherwise had never seen parts of their country. Wood engravings from the book were copied and duplicated in various forms and in other publications, giving them even wider circulation. James D. Smillie, an artist hired by the publishers of *Picturesque America* to render scenes of the valley, followed in the tradition of painters such as Albert Bierstadt. He used dramatic light and clouds to enhance the natural grandeur of the valley's features. These hand-colored versions, similar to ones sold throughout the late nineteenth century, present an untamed, ethereal place, unmarked by the hand of man.

TENAYA CANON, FROM GLACIER POINT.

YOSEMITE FALL.

Two examples from the 1870s illustrating two contrasting faces of Yosemite Falls. Above is the work of James Smillie for *Picturesque America,* and at right, the same scene illustrated for *Harper's Weekly.* Today, even after hundreds of books and countless thousands of photographs of Yosemite have been produced and reproduced, the valley's splendor never ceases to inspire and amaze.

THE YOSEMITE FALLS.

The editors wish to thank Gary F. Kurutz, Curator of the California
State Library, and Kathleen Manning of Prints Old and Rare.

The prints herein are produced from originals, courtesy of the California
State Library, pages 9-57, 62, 66, 67,72; and courtesy of Prints Old and
Rare, pages 60, 68-71. In some cases the prints have been enlarged or
reduced to fit this format, and discolorations, creases, and minor defects
have been eliminated digitally. Reproduction of the whole or any part of
the contents without written permission is prohibited.